CONTENTS

INTRODUCTION

This book is packed full of crafting ideas to equip your little superheroes with everything they need to save the day! It's all here—from reversible masks and capes that flip between different identities in the blink of an eye, to jetpacks, arm cuffs, and wooden spoon puppets (complete with their own mini removable capes). We even show you how to throw the perfect superhero party, with a fantastic cake and ideas for food, games, and party decor.

All of the projects featured are straightforward to make, with simple instructions and accompanying photos for every step, along with handy tips. Throughout the book, we've used easy-to-source materials and ensured the projects can be made by children with adult supervision and perhaps a little assistance, depending on the age of your child.

All the crafts made have been tried and tested on our own little superheroes—we have four of them at home, so every single project in this book has been put through its paces with their super strength and speed. Kids can destroy things very quickly, so we try to create projects that will stand the test of time and be loved for as long as they want to love them. If your children have a favorite superhero, or want to invent their own, all the projects can be adapted easily to reflect the colors or looks they like.

We really hope your little ones have fun using this book to transform themselves into their own wonderful and colorful superheroes.

Happy superhero crafting!

TOOLS AND MATERIALS

The good news is that you can create the superhero look without loads of materials. But there are a few items that are essential for the projects, some that are useful, and others that are just great to have around when crafting with kids! These are all detailed below.

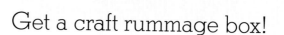

Sewing supplies

★ Felt—by far the best material for sewing with kids. It's easy to work with, doesn't fray, and is cheap and colorful.

★ Fake leather—we use this with some of the projects featured as it gives a great superhero effect and is nice and cheap. All the leather projects can be substituted with felt if you prefer though.

★ Iron-on adhesive—this interfacing cleverly sticks two pieces of fabric together once ironed, making appliqués super easy.

★ Sewing machine—not an essential, but a good time saver, particularly for the cape and shorts featured in this book.

Get a craft rummage box!

We recommend you find yourself a large box and gradually fill it up with old cartons, lids, card, fabric scraps, and anything else you think has an interesting shape or color. Kids LOVE having a craft box to rummage through, and you might be surprised at the amazing things they can produce when left to their own devices with a box of materials, some double-sided tape, and maybe a smidgen of glitter....

Craft essentials

★ Permanent colored markers—these are great for adding stay-on color without having to dig out the paints.

★ Duct tape—waterproof, strong, and comes in a wide range of colors, making it great for adding pattern and color to projects.

★ Craft foam—a durable alternative to card and a fantastic thing to have around for kids' crafting in general.

★ Glue gun—obviously not one for the kiddies, but for a quick-drying, strong hold this is a really useful item to have on hand.

★ Double-sided tape—essential for kids' crafts, it's a no-mess, instant-stick, child-friendly option.

REVERSIBLE CAPE

This super-easy cape features star and lightning bolt emblems, but you could make it to resemble your favorite superheroes/villains, or create two new characters with personalized emblems featuring your initials. The project requires a sewing machine—you could make it without one but it will take you a while to stitch around the edges!

You will need

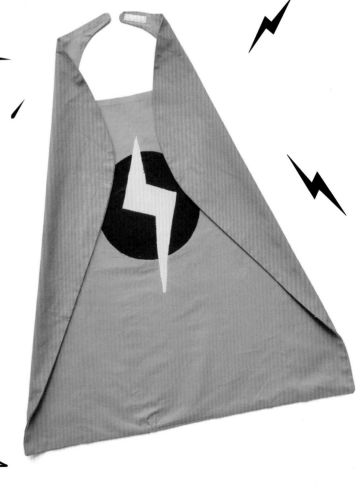

★ 1yd (1m) square each of green and blue cotton

★ 4in (10cm) square each of red and black cotton

★ 8in (20cm) square of yellow cotton

★ Scissors

★ Sewing needle and pins

★ 15 x 35in (38 x 90cm) of fusible webbing

★ Sewing machine and matching thread

★ 1½ x ½in (4 x 1cm) of Velcro/hook-and-loop tape

★ Iron and ironing board

Step 1

Photocopy the cape template (see below) and cut it out. Fold your green fabric in half and pin the template on top. Cut out one cape then repeat with the blue fabric. Use a side plate (about 8in/20cm) to draw and cut out a circle from yellow and black cotton. If you want to use the emblems featured here, cut out a yellow lightning bolt and a red star shape—draw your own or use the templates on page 10 and increase the size. Also cut the circles, lightning, and star shapes out of fusible webbing.

Step 2

Iron the fusible webbing onto the back of each shape. Line up the yellow circle centrally on the front of the blue cape 8in (20cm) from the neckline. Iron in place, and then iron the star on top of the center of the yellow circle. Repeat with the green cape, the black circle, and the lightning bolt.

Step 3

Pin the two capes right sides together. Machine sew around the edge with a ½in (1cm) seam allowance. Leave a 6in (15cm) gap along the bottom to allow you to turn the cape right sides out. Trim the edges around the neckline of the cape then make snips in the seam allowance around the curved edges, about 1in (2.5cm) apart. This will prevent puckering.

Step 4

Turn the cape right sides out and push out all the corners and neckline. Press the cape and sew the turning gap closed by hand.

Step 5

Pin and sew one piece of the Velcro onto the end of the neckline on the blue fabric. Sew the other piece on the green fabric (at the other side) so that the two pieces line up when the neckline is joined.

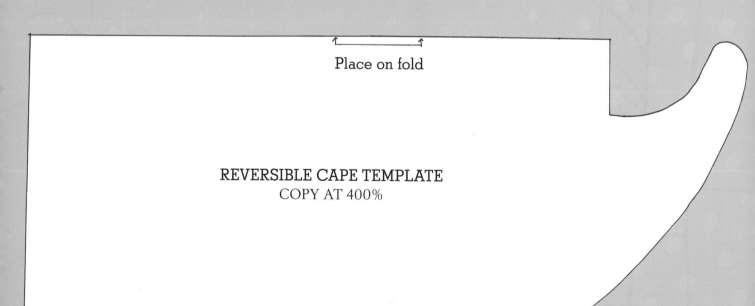

Place on fold

REVERSIBLE CAPE TEMPLATE
COPY AT 400%

1

To get children interested in sewing, let them sit on your knees while you use a sewing machine. They can help guide the fabric as you sew.

2

3

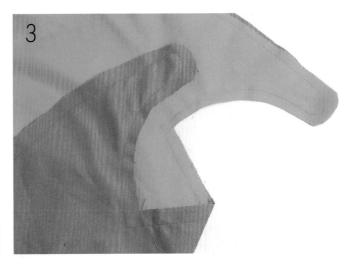

4

5

SUPERHERO MASK

Every superhero needs to conceal their true identity from the world. This reversible mask is easy to make from felt and will allow you to flip between your two chosen characters in the blink of an eye.

You will need

★ 9 x 4in (23 x 10cm) each of red and green felt

★ 9 x 4in (23 x 10cm) of fusible interfacing

★ Scrap of yellow felt

★ Scissors

★ About 15in (38cm) of thin elastic

★ Yellow embroidery thread, sewing needle and pins

★ Iron and ironing board

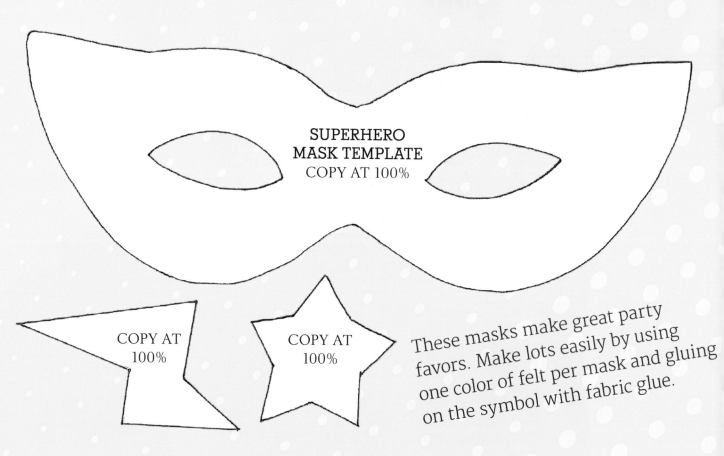

SUPERHERO
MASK TEMPLATE
COPY AT 100%

COPY AT
100%

COPY AT
100%

These masks make great party favors. Make lots easily by using one color of felt per mask and gluing on the symbol with fabric glue.

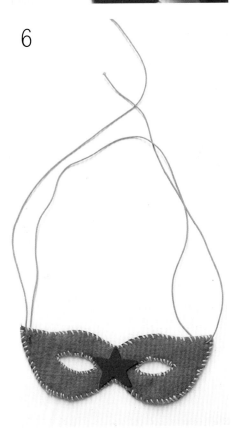

Step 1

Use the template opposite to cut mask shapes from red and green felt. Cut a star from red felt and fusible interfacing, and a lightning bolt from yellow felt and fusible interfacing.

Step 2

Following the manufacturer's instructions, attach the fusible interfacing onto the lightning bolt and star, using a cloth to protect the felt from melting. Remove the backing from the interfacing.

Step 3

Press the star onto the side of the green mask and the lightning onto the red mask.

Step 4

Pin the two masks together with the symbols on the outside. Hand sew around the outside of the mask and inside the eye holes with yellow embroidery thread.

Step 5

Use a sharp pair of scissors to pierce a hole at the top of the mask on either side.

Step 6

Thread the elastic through the mask at both sides, fit on your superhero's head, and secure with a knot.

SUPERHERO ARM CUFFS

Arm cuffs add the finishing touches to any superhero's outfit. These cuffs are made from fake leather, which is easy to work with as it doesn't fray, but if you prefer you could use felt. These cuffs have been sewn with a sewing machine, but if you don't have one or are short on time you can glue the fabric together.

You will need:

★ 10 x 8in (25 x 20cm) of gold fake leather or felt

★ 8 x 6in (20 x 15cm) of red fake leather or felt

★ Scissors

★ Masking tape

★ Tracing paper or baking parchment

★ Sewing machine and matching thread

★ Fabric glue

★ 2 x 4in (10cm) strips of Velcro/hook-and-loop tape

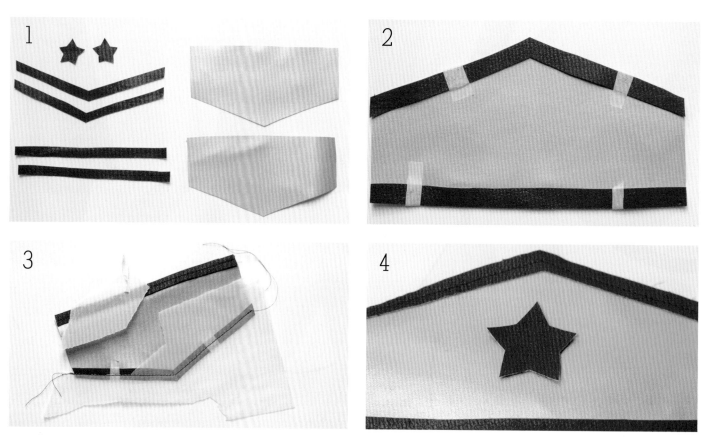

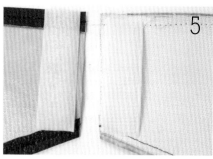

Once you've made arm cuffs you could make leg cuffs and a matching belt in a similar style.

Step 1

Photocopy the template opposite and use to cut out two arm cuffs from gold fake leather and the trim from red fake leather. Use the template on page 10 to cut out the stars from the red fake leather.

Step 2

Use small pieces of masking tape to hold the trim in place on the bottom and top of each cuff.

Step 3

To stop the fabric sticking while you are sewing, place a piece of tracing paper or baking parchment over the top of the cuff and machine sew the trim in place. Once finished, gently tear off the paper and peel away the masking tape.

Step 4

Glue the stars in the middle of the cuffs using fabric glue.

Step 5

Place one half of the Velcro strip on the back of one of the cuffs at the narrow end, and the other on the front at the other end. Machine sew in place and repeat for the other cuff.

SUPERHERO ARM CUFFS
COPY AT 100%

Choose very simple
shapes like stars

and lightning bolts
to make striking

emblems for your
superhero arm cuffs!

MAGIC SHIELD

Fend off attacks from evil villains with this simple duct tape shield. Decorate with the symbols used in this book or design your own using any shape and color you prefer.

You will need:

★ 3 x 17in (45cm) squares of corrugated cardboard

★ Scissors

★ PVA glue

★ Gold duct tape

★ 12 x 3in (30 x 8cm) strip of blue craft foam

★ 1 x sheet of blue card, 12 x 16in (30 x 40cm)

★ 1 x sheet each of red and yellow card, 8 x 12in (20 x 30cm)

★ Glue stick

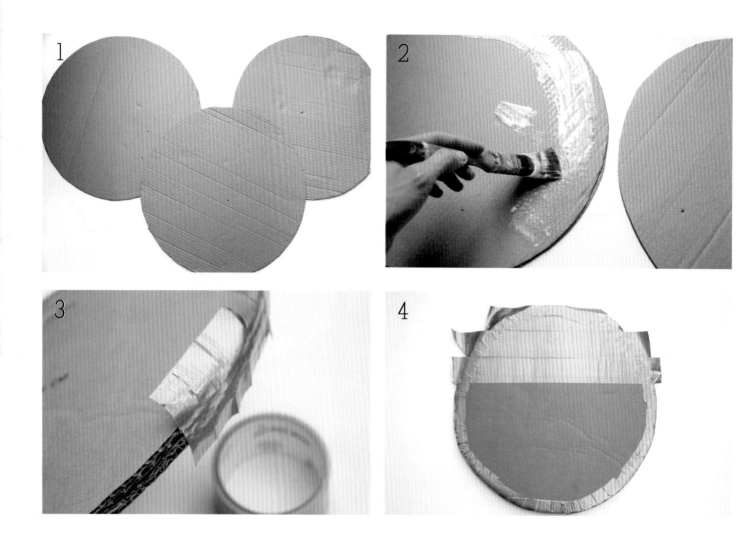

Step 1

Draw a circle about 15in (38cm) in diameter onto one of the squares of corrugated card. Cut out then repeat to make two more cardboard circles.

Step 2

Use PVA glue to fix the three pieces of cardboard together.

Step 3

Cover the edges of the shield with the duct tape by attaching strips of tape approximately 12in (30cm) long along the edge of the shield. Cut vertical snips into the tape down to the shield edge and fold down the tabs to create an even finish.

Step 4

Cover both sides of the shield with long strips of duct tape. Trim the excess tape to create a neat edge around the shield.

Step 5

Draw an 11in (28cm) diameter circle onto blue card and an 8in (20cm) diameter circle onto yellow card, then cut out. Cut out a star shape from red card (you can use the story stones template on page 62). Glue the larger circle onto the center of the shield, followed by the smaller circle and star on top, using the glue stick. If you like, you can use black and green circles and a lightning shape.

Step 6

To make the handle, take the strip of craft foam and bend it into a C shape. Use duct tape to attach the ends onto the back of the shield in the center.

Duct tape is great for crafting because it's strong, bright, and tearable. If you want neater edges, cut the tape with scissors with blades that have been rubbed with soapy water (or the blades will get sticky!)

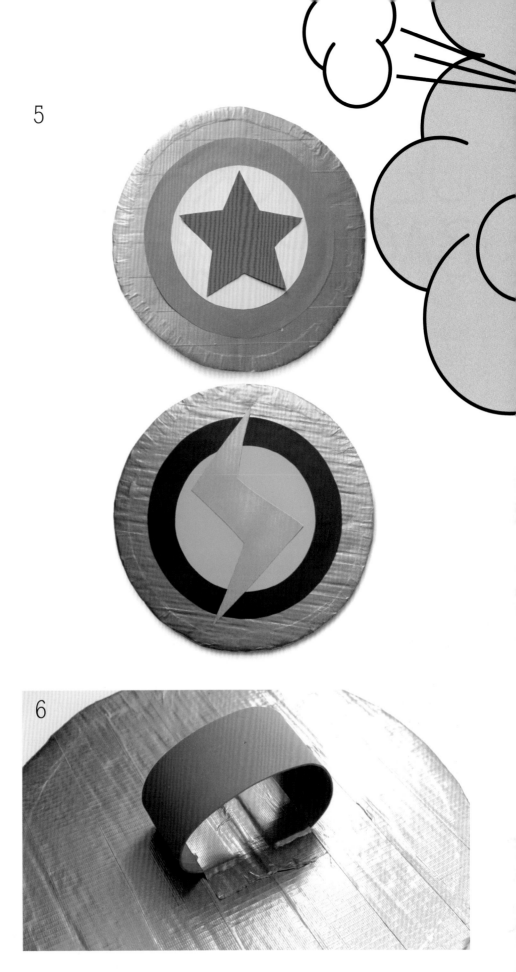

5

6

JETPACK BACKPACK

If flying isn't your super power, have no fear!
This jetpack can get superheroes to the scene
of the crime in no time. The pack doubles up as
a backpack to store snacks, drinks, and all other
superhero essentials.

You will need:

★ 1 x shoebox with a lid, approx. 12 x 7in
(30 x 18cm)

★ Red acrylic paint

★ Paintbrush

★ Scissors

★ Gold duct tape

★ 1 x sheet each of blue and red craft foam,
8 x 12in (20 x 30cm)

★ Mixture of bottle tops and lids

★ 3 x small plastic plant pots (about
2in/5cm diameter)

★ Strong glue

★ Gold spray paint

★ Red, orange, and yellow tissue paper

★ 50in (1.3m) of 1in (2.5cm)-thick
cotton tape

★ Masking tape

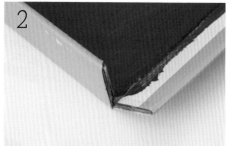

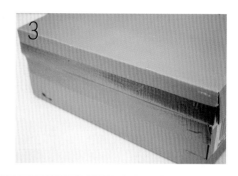

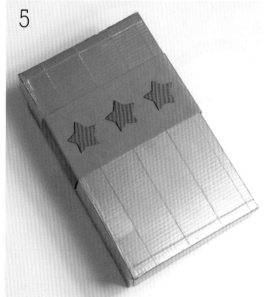

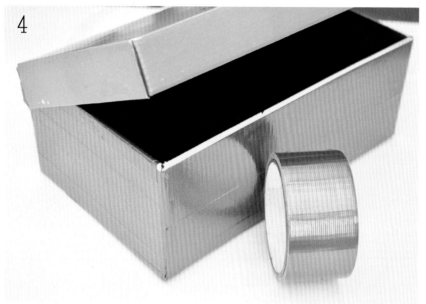

Step 1

Paint the inside of the shoe box and lid with several coats of red paint. Leave to dry.

Step 2

Make a cut in both corners of one of the long sides of the box lid to create an opening for the pack.

Step 3

Use duct tape to stick the lid flap you have created onto the top of the shoe box. Attach another piece of duct tape along the inside edge to keep the lid in place.

Step 4

Open up the lid and cover the outside of the lid and box with strips of gold duct tape.

Step 5

For the decoration, cut a 4in (10cm) strip of blue craft foam from the length of the sheet. Cut out three stars from the red craft foam sheet (you can use the template on page 10). Glue the blue strip onto the front of the jetpack, about 2½in (7cm) from the top. Trim the edges to line up with the lid of the box. Glue the stars on top.

6

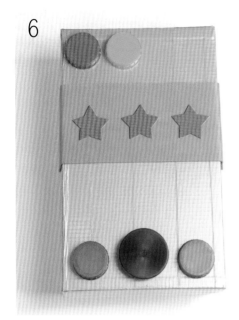

7

8

Step 6

Arrange bottle tops and lids on the front and top of the jetpack and glue in place to look like buttons.

Step 7

Spray paint the plant pots gold and leave to dry. Cut the yellow, orange, and red tissue paper into spikes and glue these spikes inside the rim of each pot. Then glue the pots onto the bottom of the jetpack.

Step 8

For the straps, cut the cotton tape in half and fold each piece into a loop. Place the loops alongside each other on the back of the backpack with the ends overlapping underneath. Tape them on temporarily with masking tape then check the fit and adjust if necessary. Glue them in place.

SUPER-QUICK OUTFIT

This little set is so easy to make using a bit of fake leather, some felt, and a leotard—or you could decorate a T-shirt instead. The outfit goes really well with the Superhero Arm Cuffs on page 12 or the Easy-Sew Shorts on page 36.

For the crown you will need:

★ 4 x 10in (10 x 25cm) of gold fake leather

★ Scrap of red fake leather

★ Scissors

★ Fabric glue

★ Sewing machine and matching thread

★ 10in (25cm) of 1in (2.5cm)-thick white elastic

For the leotard you will need:

★ Leotard

★ 9in (23cm) square of yellow felt

★ 4in (10cm) square of blue felt

★ Fabric glue

★ Yellow embroidery thread and needle

★ Pins

CROWN
COPY AT 100%

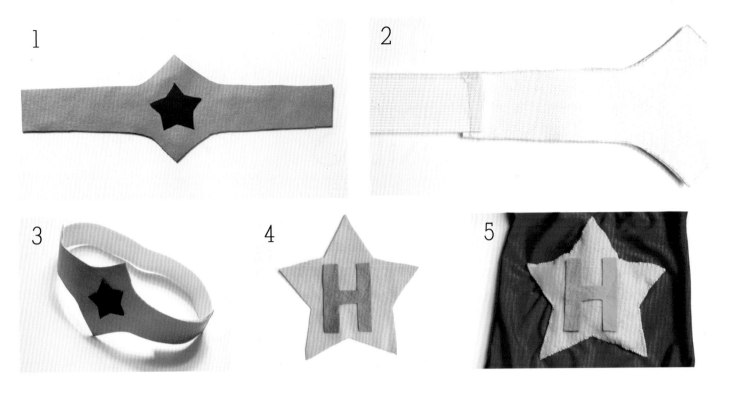

1

2

3   4   5

Step 1

Use the template opposite to cut out the crown from gold leather. Then cut out a star from red leather. Glue the star onto the center of the crown with fabric glue and leave to dry.

Step 2

Machine sew one end of the elastic onto the back of one end of the crown, with a ½in (1cm) overlap.

Step 3

Wrap the crown onto your child's head so that it fits snugly, then mark and sew the other end to the crown where measured. Cut the excess elastic inside the crown.

Step 4

Cut out a large star from yellow felt (you can use the story stones template on page 62 for this). Draw your initial onto blue felt so it's approximately 3½in (9cm) high. Cut out and glue the initial onto the center of the star.

Step 5

Pin the star onto the front of the leotard in the middle, then hand sew in place with yellow embroidery thread using whipstitch (see right).

Whipstitch

This simple decorative stitch is used to sew two pieces of fabric together. Knot the thread and pull the needle through from behind the top piece of fabric to conceal the knot. Bring the needle back through from the bottom piece to the top, stitching over the edge of the fabric. Continue all the way around the fabric.

POW! BAM! ACCESSORIES

Kaboom! These hair clips are made from sparkly craft foam, which is a fantastic material for crafting with kids. It's easy to cut, weatherproof, and comes in great colors. You can make all sorts of jewelry from it, but here we've made some hair clips, along with a matching necklace from shrink plastic.

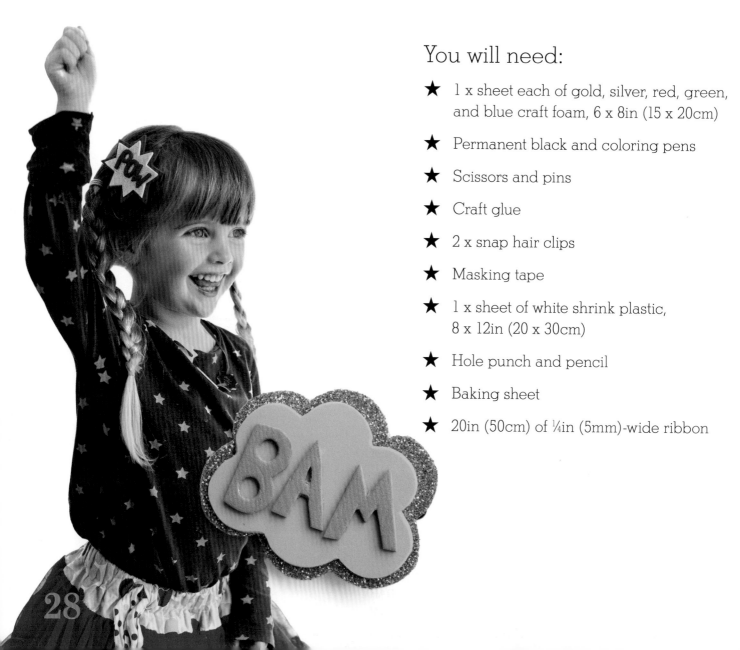

You will need:

★ 1 x sheet each of gold, silver, red, green, and blue craft foam, 6 x 8in (15 x 20cm)

★ Permanent black and coloring pens

★ Scissors and pins

★ Craft glue

★ 2 x snap hair clips

★ Masking tape

★ 1 x sheet of white shrink plastic, 8 x 12in (20 x 30cm)

★ Hole punch and pencil

★ Baking sheet

★ 20in (50cm) of ¼in (5mm)-wide ribbon

Step 1

Draw and cut out an explosive shape from blue craft foam, measuring roughly 2½ x 2in (6 x 5cm). Place it onto a silver piece of foam and draw around it, then cut out the silver shape so that it is about ¼in (5mm) smaller than the blue one. Repeat with other colors and shapes.

Step 2

Write some superhero phrases onto another sheet of craft foam and cut out. Note that the phrases will need to fit inside the smallest foam shape, so you could draw the shape onto the foam sheet to make it easier to fit in if you like. Cut the foam letters out.

Step 3

Line up the text on the small shape and glue in place. Glue the small shape onto the bigger one and leave to dry.

Step 4

Cut a 1½ x ¾in (4 x 2cm) strip of foam and feed the hair clip onto it. Glue onto the back of the foam shapes. You can use masking tape to hold it in place if necessary. Once dry, gently remove the tape.

Step 5

To make the necklace, draw some superhero phrases onto shrink plastic in pencil. Each one should measure about 3 x 2in (8 x 5cm). Give the phrases an explosive double border to match the hair clips. Once you are happy with the drawings, go over the lines with permanent black pen.

Step 6

Color the drawings in using permanent coloring pens (or the color will leak out). Remember that the colors will darken when they shrink, so try and pick lighter tones. Use a hole punch to make holes on each side of the plastic.

The hair clips—which could also be turned into badges—make great party favors.

Step 7

Place the shrink plastic on a baking sheet and follow the manufacturer's instructions to shrink the plastic in the oven. Remove and leave to cool, then thread the shapes onto a piece of ribbon and tie it so that it fits over your child's head easily.

BIG UTILITY BELT

This belt is a superhero's best friend, with a hook for a torch and hidden pockets for maps, pens, and money (even superheroes need pocket money!) Large sheets of felt can be purchased from online retailers or good craft stores.

You will need:

★ 12 x 40in (30 x 100cm) of thick yellow felt

★ 8½in (22cm) square of bright blue felt

★ Scissors

★ Sewing machine and matching thread

★ Tailor's chalk/pencil

★ 2 x strips of Velcro/hook-and-loop tape, 3in (8cm) long

★ Blue carabiner clip

Step 1

Photocopy the belt template on page 62 and cut it out. Fold the yellow felt in half, pin the template on top and draw around it. Extend the sides as long as you need to be able to fit around the child's waist with roughly a 3in (8cm) overlap. Photocopy the belt logo on page 62 and cut out. Cut the belt logo shape out of blue felt. Using the template below, draw and cut your initial letter out of blue felt so that it fits inside the belt logo.

Step 2

Arrange the letter onto the middle of the belt with the blue belt logo on top, then pin in place and machine sew along the edge of the felt.

Step 3

Cut two rectangles measuring 3½ x 5in (9 x 13cm) and a 2½ x 5in (6 x 13cm) triangle from yellow felt. Pin the rectangles on either side of the logo. Machine sew in place around the sides and bottom edge, just inside the edge of the felt, to make pockets. On one of the pockets, sew another line 1½in (4cm) from the side to create a pen holder.

Step 4

Pin the felt triangle at the top of the other pocket, with the base of the triangle ¼in (5mm) from the top of the pocket. The triangle should point down over the pocket, like an envelope. Machine sew along the base of the triangle, making sure you do not stitch over the pocket opening. You now have two pockets, one either side of the emblem.

Step 5

Cut a 2 x ½in (5 x 1cm) strip of yellow felt. Fold it in half and pin to the back of the belt just under one of the pockets. Pin with a ½in (1cm) overlap, with the loop hanging down. Machine sew in place.

ALPHABET
COPY AT 200%

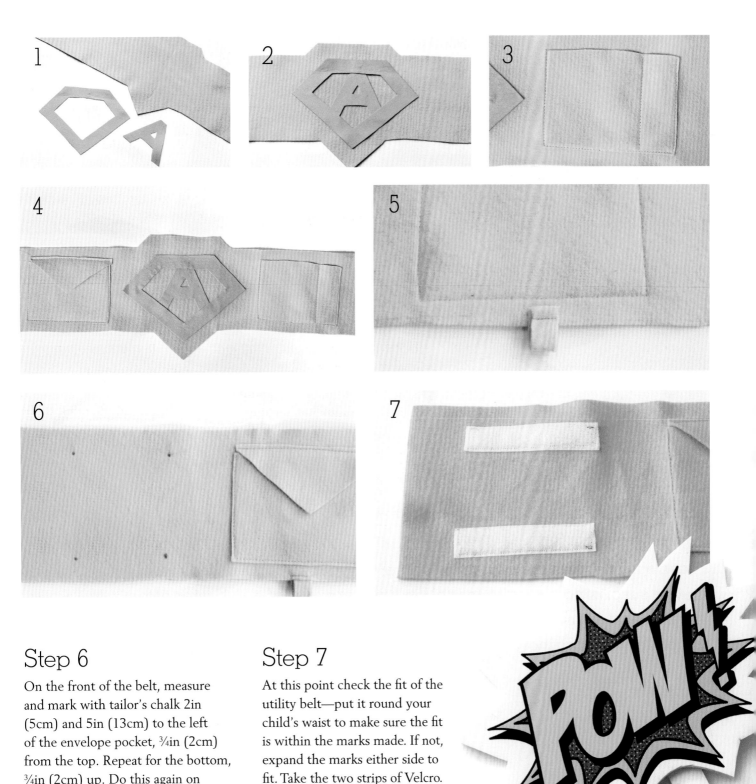

Step 6

On the front of the belt, measure and mark with tailor's chalk 2in (5cm) and 5in (13cm) to the left of the envelope pocket, ¾in (2cm) from the top. Repeat for the bottom, ¾in (2cm) up. Do this again on the other side, but this time on the reverse of the belt.

Step 7

At this point check the fit of the utility belt—put it round your child's waist to make sure the fit is within the marks made. If not, expand the marks either side to fit. Take the two strips of Velcro. Pin the fluffy sides onto one side of the belt and the scratchy sides on the other side, between each of the marks. Machine sew in place. Cut away the excess felt on the belt. Attach the carabiner clip to the loop.

EASY-SEW SHORTS

These starry shorts are perfect to complete your superhero look, and they're surprisingly easy to make! This pattern will fit a 4–6 year old —if you want to make the shorts bigger or smaller, enlarge or reduce the pattern accordingly.

You will need:

★ ½yd (½m) of starry blue cotton fabric

★ Scissors

★ Tailor's chalk

★ Pins

★ Iron and ironing board

★ Sewing machine and matching thread

★ 78in (2m) of ½in (1cm)-wide red bias binding tape

★ 60in (1.5m) of ¼in (5mm)-wide cord

★ Small safety pin

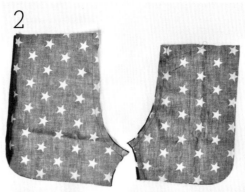

Step 1

Photocopy the templates on page 64 and cut them out. Fold the fabric in half, pin the front and back templates onto the fabric, and cut out two front and two back pieces. At this point you may find it useful to mark the front pieces with a piece of tape or tailor's chalk, as they do look quite similar when sewn!

Step 2

Pin the two front pieces right sides together and sew the inner curved edges, as shown on the photo, using a ½in (1cm) seam allowance (use this seam allowance for all the pieces). Repeat for the back pieces.

Step 3

Open out the pieces you have just sewn together. Pin the front and back pieces right sides together and sew the crotch area together. Press the seams open.

Step 4

Starting at the top edge of the front of the shorts, encase the raw edges with bias binding and pin in place. Pin the binding all the way around the front of the shorts and a third of the way up the back.

Step 5

Cut the remaining binding off and repeat for the other side of the shorts. Sew in place along the center of the bias binding.

Step 6

Overlap the front edges of the shorts onto the back edges, so that the binding and back raw edges are concealed inside the shorts.

Step 7

Pin and sew the sides down the previous stitch line along the binding. Start from the top of the shorts and stop once you reach the curved edges. Repeat for the other side.

Step 8

Press the top of the shorts over by ½in (1cm), then press again by ¾in (2cm) to create a channel for the cord. Pin in place. Measure and mark ⅛in (3mm) and ⅝in (1.5cm) from the top fold, along the center seam on the front of the shorts.

Step 9

Unpin the fold and open up the top of the shorts. Sew a box around the seam, along your marks and ¼in (5mm) from the seam. Unpick the seam to create an opening. Re-pin the fold and sew all the way around the channel, along the fold.

Step 10

Attach a small safety pin to the end of the length of cord. Feed it in through the opening in the channel and ease it all the way around and out the other side. Make small knots in both ends of the cord to secure.

SUPERSONIC CAR

This car makes the perfect centerpiece to a superhero party (see page 56 for some great party ideas). It is made from three large cardboard boxes, but you could use one box and lots of spare card instead. You can paint the car blue like we have here or keep it unpainted. It does require a fair amount of paint—a small pot from a hardware store is a cheaper option than craft paint.

You will need:

★ 3 x large cardboard boxes, each approx. 18 x 30in (46 x 76cm)

★ Masking tape

★ Scissors and craft knife

★ Tape measure or ruler

★ Blue and yellow paint

★ 3 x sheets of red card, 8 x 12in (20 x 30cm)

★ 2 x sheets of yellow and black card, 8 x 12in (20 x 30cm)

★ 1 x sheet of orange card, 8 x 12in (20 x 30cm)

★ PVA glue

★ Cardboard tube

★ A few colorful bottle tops

★ Acetate, approx. 17 x 7in (43 x 18cm)

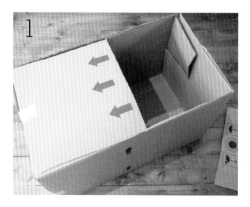

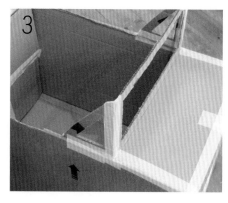

Step 1

Take one of the cardboard boxes and secure all the flaps with masking tape. Using the craft knife, cut down the center of one of the long sides of the box, then cut around the edges, leaving one of the narrow ends attached, to create a large flap.

Step 2

Measure about 8in (20cm) from the fold on the flap. Score a line across at this point and fold the cardboard up. Cut out the center of this section, with a 1in (2.5cm) border all the way around, to make the windshield.

Step 3

Cut two right-angle triangles 8 x 6in (20 x 15cm) from spare cardboard. Cut the centers out as before with a 1in (2.5cm) border. Use masking tape to attach these triangles to each side of the windshield and onto the sides of the box.

Step 4

Cut two quarter circles from the cardboard that are the same height as your car. Tape them to the front of the box to make the front panels.

Step 5

Connect the front panels by taping a piece of cardboard, cut to fit, between them. Cut the cardboard so that you can bend it to curve around the panels.

Step 6

Cut two back panels from cardboard, curved upward as shown, and attach to the back of the box in the same way as the front panels. Cut two booster shapes from cardboard and tape inside each back panel.

Step 7

Cut a door into one side of the car, all the way to the bottom and about 12in (30cm) across, making sure you leave one side attached for a hinge. Paint the outside of the car blue, with yellow boosters, and leave to dry. You will probably want to take it outside onto the grass for this bit to avoid mess!

Step 8

Cut a logo from colored card. We've gone for a yellow lightning bolt in a red circle, but you could use your initials or a superhero symbol. Glue onto the side of the car.

Step 9

Cut four wheels from black card. Cut small symbols to match the one on the side of the car. Glue the symbols in the center of the wheels, then glue the wheels onto the car.

Step 10

Cut a sheet of yellow card in half across the width. Curve the edges of the card and glue to the front of the car for headlamps.

Step 11

Cut flames from red and yellow card and glue to the boosters.

Step 12

Cut a piece of acetate to fit the windshield. Cut two lightning bolt shapes from yellow card and glue onto the acetate to make windshield wipers. Glue inside the windshield.

Step 13

Finally, paint a cardboard tube yellow and glue it onto the top of the car door to make a handle. Glue a selection of bottle tops inside the car—you can add labels such as "go" and "stop" if you like.

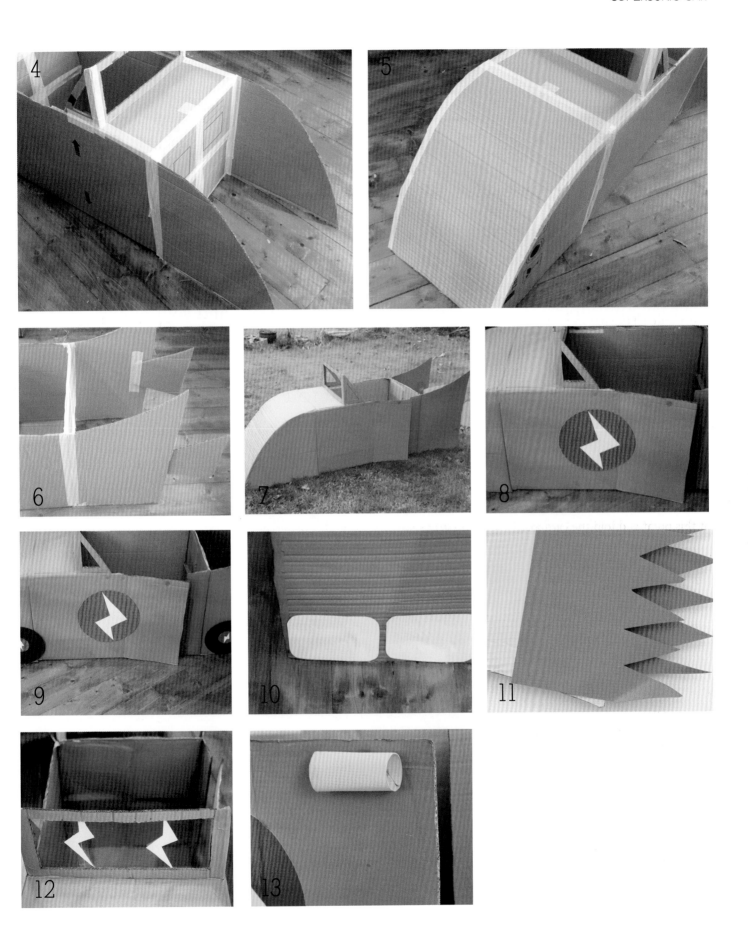

SUPERHERO SPOON PUPPETS

These cute puppets are made from a set of wooden spoons and they feature detachable capes and masks so that they can be superheroes or keep their identity secret. You can make the ones featured here or adapt them to make your favorite superheroes—or even a super version of you and your family!

You will need

★ 4 x wooden spoons

★ Acrylic paint in pale pink, brown, white, yellow, red, and gray

★ Paintbrush

★ 1 x sheet each of red, black, yellow, blue, and green felt, 6 x 8in (15 x 20cm)

★ Scissors and embroidery needle

★ Craft glue

★ Pencil and eraser

★ Black, red, and pink marker pens

★ Orange, yellow, and black yarn

★ 1 x book, approx. 10 x 8in (25 x 20cm)

★ 6in (15cm) of fine elastic

★ ¼ x ½in (0.5 x 1cm) of Velcro/hook-and-loop tape

Step 1

Paint the top of the spoons your desired skin tone color—use pale pink as a base and mix it with a little white, yellow, or brown paint. Paint the sticks of the spoons to make the bodies—paint two spoons red, one gray, and one blue and leave to dry.

Step 2

Photocopy the templates on page 63 and use to cut a mask and cape each from blue and green felt, a bat mask and cape from black felt, a cape and star from red felt, and a crown from yellow. Glue the star onto the crown.

Step 3

Place the masks onto the spoons and mark where the eyeholes are onto three of the spoons in pencil: the black mask onto the gray spoon, the blue mask onto the blue spoon, and the green mask onto one red spoon.

Step 4

Draw eyes onto the spoon puppets inside the pencil markings using a black marker pen. Add a little red smile and some pink cheeks with marker pens, then rub out the pencil.

Step 5

For the ponytail hair, wrap the orange wool around the width of a book about 40 times. Pull it off and tie it in the center with another strand of wool. Cut through the loops to make a loose pompom. Open one side of the pompom out and glue onto the top of the head of one of the red spoons. Glue the strands at the back onto the spoon and trim the front to make a fringe.

Step 6

For the long hair, wrap yellow wool about 40 times round the length of the book. Tie in the center, cut the loops, and glue onto the top of the other red spoon so that the knotted center resembles a parting. Glue the strands down on the back and sides of the head and trim the ends.

Step 7

To make short hair, wrap the black wool round the width of the book about 20 times. Knot the center, then cut the strands as before. Glue on top of the blue spoon, at the side, to create a parting. Glue the strands down and repeat with the orange hair onto the gray spoon.

Step 8

Push the length of elastic through both sides of one of the masks, using a needle. Place it onto the puppet and tie in place to fit. Repeat for the other masks and crown.

Step 9

Take the strip of Velcro and glue each side onto the top of the cape.

Step 10

Paint little emblems onto the front of each puppet to give them an identity. This could be anything you like!

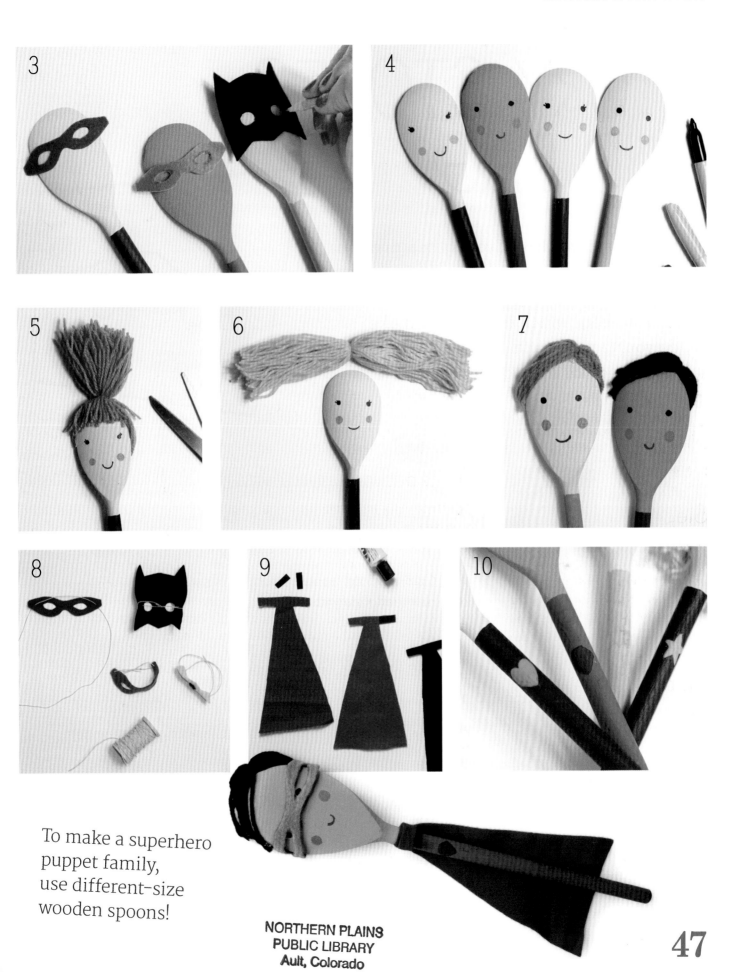

To make a superhero
puppet family,
use different-size
wooden spoons!

STORY STONES AND BAG

This is a great way to get young imaginations flowing and a fun way to create exciting and unusual stories. These stones are kept in a drawstring bag, which is simple to make. Once you've made one bag you can make lots more—perfect for storing superhero toys in.

You will need:

★ 10 x 17in (25 x 43cm) of red cotton fabric

★ Sewing machine and matching thread

★ Scissors and pinking shears (optional)

★ 1 x 6in (15cm) square each of yellow and blue cotton fabric

★ 2 x 6in (15cm) squares of fusible interfacing

★ 20in (50cm) of ½in (1cm)-wide yellow ribbon

★ Pins and large paperclip/safety pin

★ 10–15 smooth, rounded pebbles (about 2in/5cm wide)

★ Permanent black marker pen

★ Acrylic paints and fine paintbrush or permanent colored pens

★ Craft varnish

★ Iron and ironing board

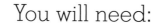

To play, simply dip your hand into the bag and pull out a stone at random. Begin a story using that character, scene or object. Continue to pull out stones and add them to your story to create a unique and often totally bizarre tale!

Step 1

Take the rectangle of red fabric and cut around the edges with pinking shears, if you have them, to prevent fraying. Fold both of the narrow ends in by ¾in (2cm) and press.

Step 2

To create the channel for the ribbon, fold over one of the long edges by ½in (1cm), then in again by 1in (2.5cm). Press and machine sew along the bottom fold.

Step 3

Fold the fabric in half widthwise with the folded edges on the outside. Pin the fabric together. Sew around the bag, starting from just underneath the sewn channel at the top, all the way around the side and bottom, with a ½in (1cm) seam allowance. Trim the bottom corners, turn out, and press.

Step 4

Place the paperclip onto the ribbon and tie it on at one end. Feed the clip into the channel of the bag, all the way to the other side.

Step 5

Iron the two squares of fusible interfacing onto the yellow and blue squares of fabric. Photocopy the templates on page 62 and cut out. Use them to draw a star onto the back of the interfacing of the blue fabric and a circle onto the back of the interfacing of the yellow fabric and cut out. Peel off the backing from the interfacing and iron the circle into the center of the bag, then iron the star on top.

Step 6

To make the story stones, give the pebbles a good clean and dry them thoroughly. Think about what you would like to have on your stones and draw them onto the pebbles using permanent marker pen. You should have a mix of characters, objects, and places.

Step 7

Paint your story stones using a fine paintbrush, or use permanent colored pens if that is easier. Then varnish the stones to seal the colors. Leave to dry and then put into the bag.

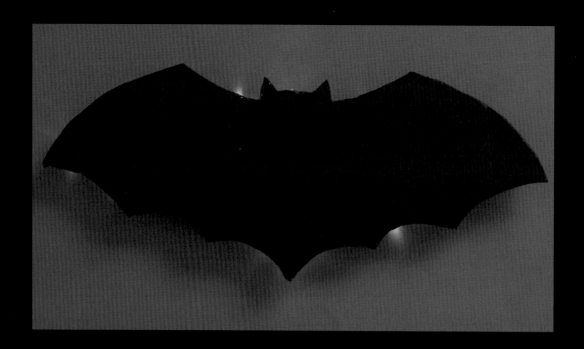

BAT NIGHT LIGHT

This bat night light gives a gentle glow while little superheroes get some shut-eye after a busy day of saving the world. You could use the bat template from page 63 or draw out your own straight onto foam board in any shape you like.

You will need:

★ 8 x 20in (20 x 50cm) fire-safe foam board

★ Craft knife

★ Artist's canvas, approx. 14 x 18in (35 x 45cm)

★ Black and blue acrylic paint

★ 8 x lengths of dowel, 1 x ½in (2.5 x 1cm)

★ Scissors

★ Battery-operated LED fairy lights

★ Strong glue

★ Sandpaper (optional)

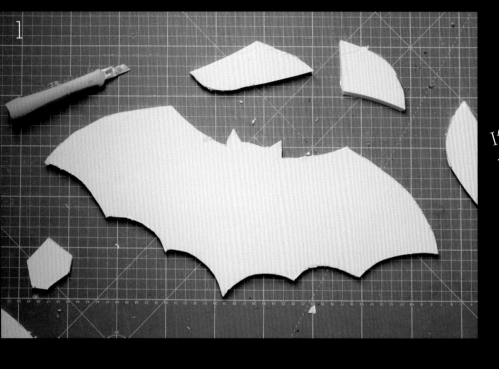

1

If you have any rough edges you can sand them gently with fine sandpaper.

Step 1

Photocopy the template on page 63 and use to draw a bat shape onto the foam board. Place onto a protective surface and cut the bat out using a

Step 4

Add glue to the end of all the pieces of dowel and glue the bat onto the center of the canvas. Hold it in place until the glue has dried.

Step 6

Feed all the lights through from the back of the canvas to the front. Spread them around so that they are evenly arranged behind the bat

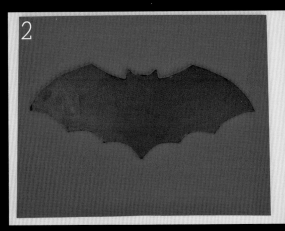

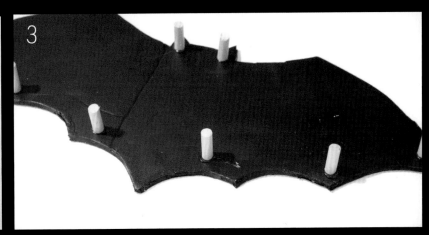

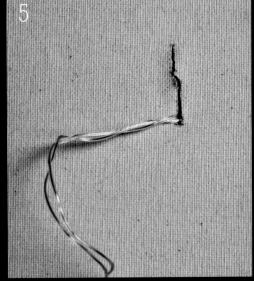

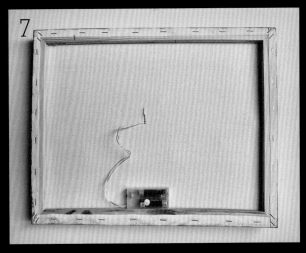

SUPERHERO PARTY

This section will provide you with top tips and ideas for throwing the most super party possible, with suggestions for food, games, and decorations. Most of the ideas can be easily adapted to fit with any theme or color scheme you fancy!

PARTY FOOD

Sandwiches
Cut into lightning-bolt shapes, or use a small star cutter to cut shapes into the bread.

Superhero emblem cupcakes
Use colored fondant icing to quickly cover cupcakes in your favorite superhero emblem.

Kryptonite jelly
Cut green jelly into jagged chunks of toxic kryptonite!

Drinks
Add a little food coloring to juice to transform it into super-power juice. Adapt the color of the juice to fit the party theme.

Cake
See page 58 for details on how to make a showstopper cake.

Power up
Jazz up food by drawing masks onto food packaging or adding paper capes to juice cartons.

DECORATION

Comic books
Use comic-book pages for place mats or roll them into cones before filling with popcorn or potato chips.

Balloons
Decorate balloons to resemble superheroes. Cut out masks from colored card and attach them to blown-up balloons using double-sided tape.

Bunting
Red, yellow, and blue are classic superhero colors. Use colored card to make the bunting and decorate with stars, lightning bolts, or letters.

GAMES & ACTIVITIES

POW! piñata
Superheroes can show off their super strength with a simple POW! piñata, made easily by gluing corrugated card together and covering in fringed crepe paper.

Superhero photo booth
Paint a large cardboard box to resemble a Pop-Art comic book. Then cut masks, tiaras, slogans, logos, etc. from card before taping onto wooden skewers to use as props.

Pin the mask on the superhero
Draw a superhero without a mask onto paper. Give each of the children a card superhero mask (name labeled!) that they can then decorate using pens, glitter, and stickers. Attach sticky tack to each one, blindfold the children and see who can get their mask in the right place. Kids can add elastic to their masks and take them home as party favors.

Craft table
Decorate cardboard tubes (cut open along the length) to make superhero cuffs. Put out bowls of stickers and card scraps, glitter, glue sticks, and felt-tip pens so the kids can create their own designs.

POW CAKE

This is a super-simple cake with a really dramatic, bright effect that will make a great centerpiece to a superhero party. If you like, you can bake the sponge cakes in advance and freeze before decorating a day or two ahead of the party.

You will need:

★ 2 cake tins measuring 10 x 8in
  (25 x 20cm)

★ 1lb 9oz (700g) superfine (caster) sugar

★ 1lb 9oz (700g) butter, at room temperature

★ 4 medium eggs

★ 17 fl oz (550ml) milk

★ 2lb (900g) self-rising flour (sifted)

★ 1lb 12oz (800g) vanilla buttercream frosting

★ 2lb 4oz (1kg) red ready-to-use fondant

★ 1lb 2oz (500g) yellow ready-to-use fondant

★ 9oz (250g) blue ready-to-use fondant

★ Rolling pin

★ Plastic wrap

Step 1

Preheat the oven to 350°F (180°C). Grease and line the tins. Cream the butter with the sugar until it is smooth and pale, then beat in the eggs, one at a time. Mix in the milk, then fold in the flour. Divide the mixture between the two tins and bake for 40–50 minutes, or until a skewer inserted into the center comes out clean.

Step 2

Remove from the tins and leave to cool completely on a wire cooling rack. If you're making in advance, cover in plastic wrap and freeze. Place the cakes next to each other and use buttercream frosting to stick together. Use the template below and a sharp knife to cut the cake into a jagged shape. Spread a layer of buttercream frosting over the cake.

Step 3

Roll the red fondant out between two layers of plastic wrap until it is about ¼in (5mm) thick and 3in (8cm) bigger than the actual cake. Remove the top layer of plastic wrap and use the bottom layer to pick the fondant up and carefully flip it over on top of the cake.

Step 4

Smooth down the fondant on top of the cake, keeping the plastic wrap in place as you do so in order not to mark it. Use your fingers to gently press the fondant between the edges of the cake. Use a sharp knife to trim off any excess fondant.

Step 5

Roll the yellow fondant out between two sheets of plastic wrap until it is about ⅛in (3mm) thick. Place the inner template on top and cut another jagged shape from the yellow fondant. Use the plastic wrap as before (see step 3) to place it on top of the cake. Smooth down, then remove the plastic wrap.

Step 6

Roll the blue fondant out between two sheets of plastic wrap until it is about ⅛in (3mm) thick and use the template to cut out the POW letters. Add a little water to the bottom of each letter and place onto the cake, starting with the 'O' in the middle to ensure the letters are central.

CAKE TEMPLATE
COPY AT 300%

1

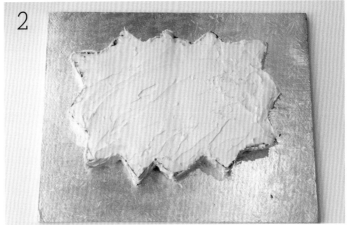
2

3

4

5

6

TEMPLATES

BIG UTILITY BELT
(see page 32)

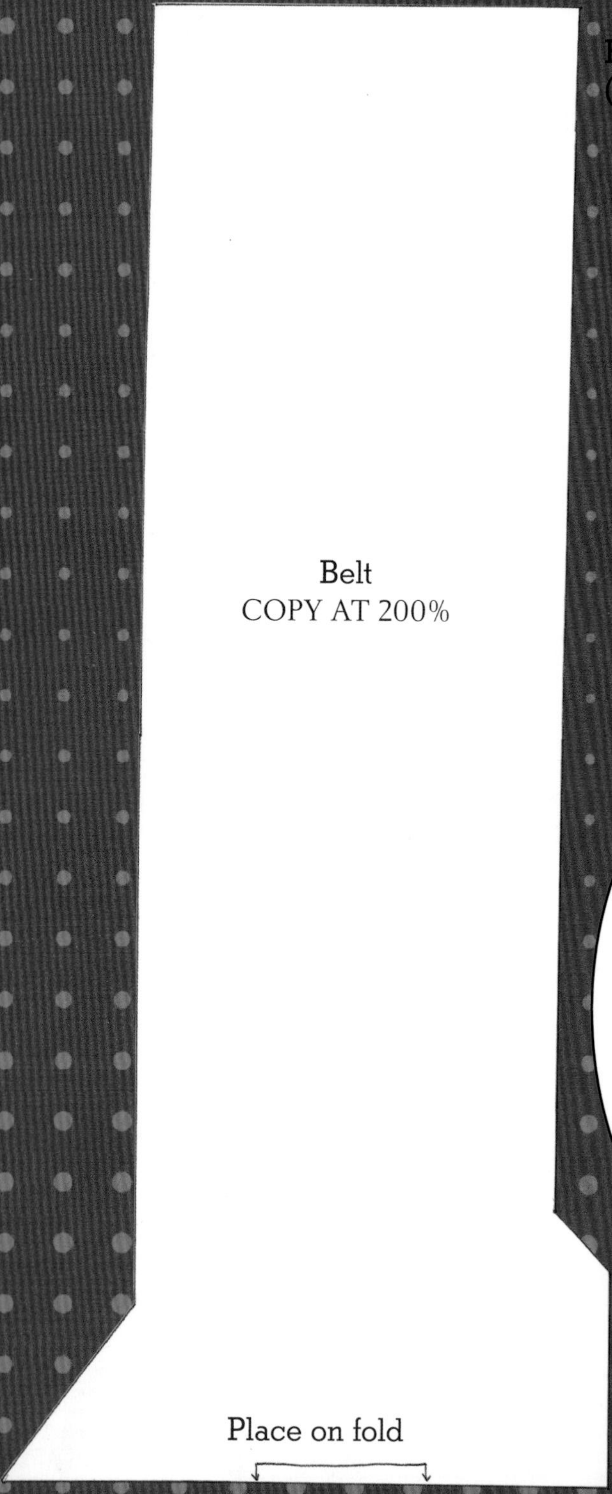

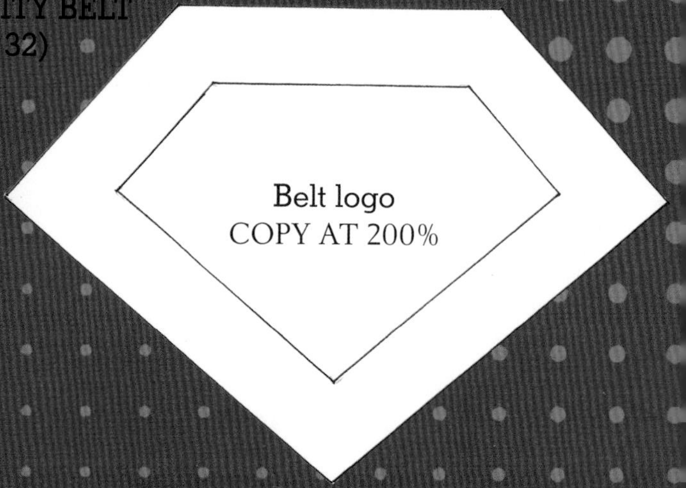

Belt logo
COPY AT 200%

Belt
COPY AT 200%

Star
COPY AT 100%

Place on fold

STORY STONES
AND BAG
(see page 48)

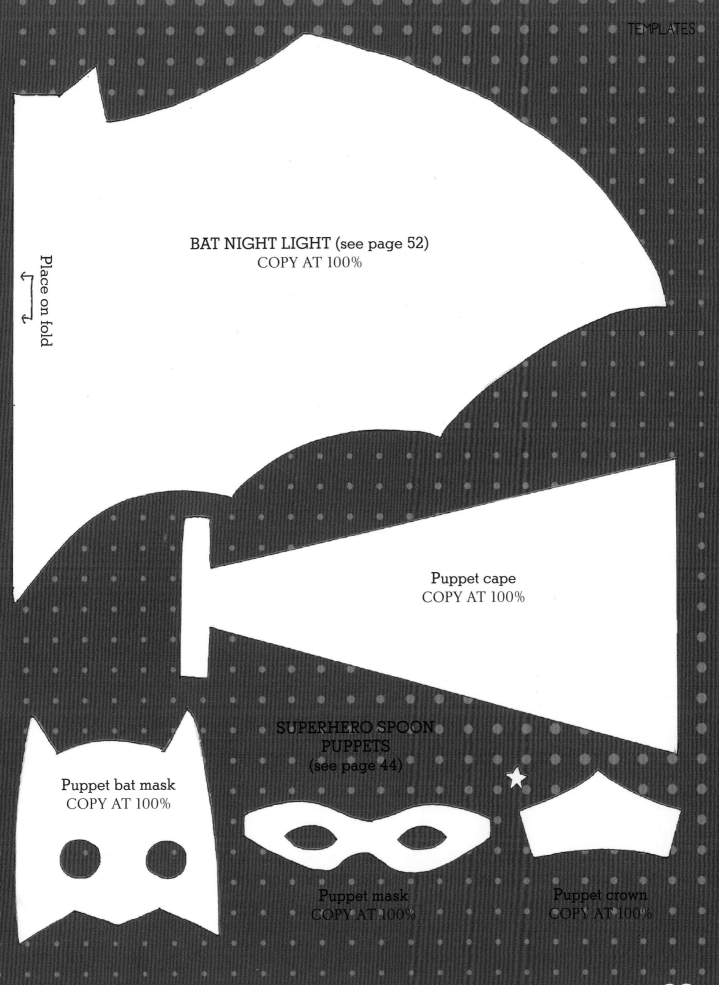

BAT NIGHT LIGHT (see page 52)
COPY AT 100%

Place on fold

Puppet cape
COPY AT 100%

SUPERHERO SPOON
PUPPETS
(see page 44)

Puppet bat mask
COPY AT 100%

Puppet mask
COPY AT 100%

Puppet crown
COPY AT 100%

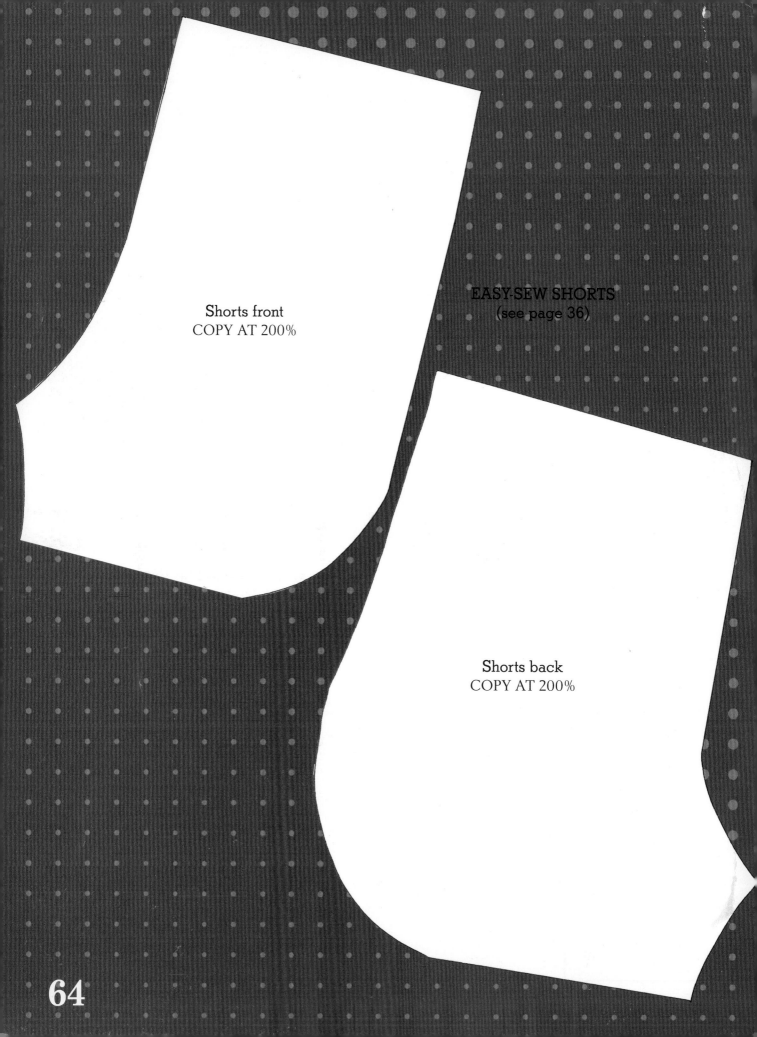

Shorts front
COPY AT 200%

EASY-SEW SHORTS
(see page 36)

Shorts back
COPY AT 200%

64